The Runes Workshop

A You know.® Intuition Workbook

The Runes Workshop

A You know.® Intuition Workbook

By Jennifer Halls

Youknow.net

You know.® LLC
Fort Mill, South Carolina

Published by:
You know.® LLC
Fort Mill, SC 29708

Comments and inquiries regarding this book may be sent to:
Jennifer@Youknow.net

ISBN-13: 978-1456587901
ISBN-10: 1456587900

Second Edition 2011
The Runes Workshop was first printed in a slightly
different version in the U.S. in 2009

Edited by Joanne E. Brunn and Michael Gordon
Layout by Joanne E. Brunn
Contributing Writers: Joanne E. Brunn, Ph.D. and Dianne Moore, M.ED., MFT
Photos and Illustrations by Jennifer Halls

ᚦᛖ ᛟᚾᛚᛃ ᚱᛖᚨ ᚹᚨᛚᚢᚨᛒᛚᛖ ᚦᛁᛜ ᛁᛊ ᛁᚾᛏᚢᛁᛏᛁᛟᚾ

The only real valuable thing is intuition. ***- Albert Einstein***

Table of Contents

Gratitude

With much love, gratitude and appreciation to my dear friends:

Joanne E. Brunn who cheered me on and with great patience prodded me when needed, while she did the layout and editing of this book.

Dianne Moore for reminding me how much I love the Runes.

My mother, Jean Hollister, who gave me my first set of Runes and has always enthusiastically encouraged me toward the intuitive path.

Susan Hough and Sobonfu Some' for their honesty, ever-present belief and loving insistence in telling me to write.

Jeffrey Riehm and Jenni Field who *always* lend an ear and a helping hand; and also saved my sanity by fixing my computer when it almost died two days before the book was finished.

Cynthia Fillman for creating 'emergency' PDF's and her hilarity that Magickally dispels stress.

Janet Wayland and Beth Rollison who did a bunch of work-stuff for me while I focused on the book.

All of the wonderful people I work with, especially the 2009 Rune Camp women; you inspire me and I feel more than blessed that such amazing individuals are in my life.

My family, whose humor keeps me grounded; and my dad, Larry Halls, who has always expressed his pride and support -- despite a lifelong confusion over what it is I actually do.

Those of you who live close and far, who love to laugh, tease, cry, walk, chat, share, eat, cook, dance, do ritual, boss, make art, confide, toast, pray, hug, listen, argue, watch movies, strategize, garden, trust, support, nag, gift, understand, play, swear, glitter, treasure hunt, dream and travel together with me.

And to my love, my husband Michael Gordon who encourages me to do whatever crazy thing I want to do *and* helps soft edit it all.

Foreword

In the time that I have known Jennifer, I've come to deeply value and respect her friendship, knowledge and gifts. Whenever I work with her on a project, including the layout and editing of this book, I learn something.

Some of you might browse this book and think it is a simple compilation of Rune information and exercises. Ah, but is it? The magic of Jennifer is that she makes the unusual and even the uncomfortable feel simple and painless. This 'ordinary' feeling is what allows us to enter into a space in which we can learn profound things about ourselves, our potential and the many worlds and perspectives in which we live.

As you work through this book or simply read it, relax into its words and let the energy behind them seep into you. Before you know it, you will be developing your intuition and finding insights into your life. Some of you may wonder if you are doing it right or if you are merely making it up. My advice to you, learned over many years from my friend Jennifer is to trust yourself. The more you do, the easier it will be to hear your intuition.

And most of all—have Fun!

Joanne

Joanne E. Brunn, Ph.D.
Old Greenwich, Connecticut

Introduction

My mother gave me my first set of Runes in 1986. I have used them on and off to connect to my intuition ever since. I have made countless sets for friends and spent hours filled with rich conversation initiated by the Runes. I've come to think of them as an energy that has knowledge to share. That is why they are capitalized throughout this book - to recognize their importance as less an object and something more alive.

The Runes Workshop actually came from a retreat I created in 2009. I wanted to make some handouts containing information and ideas that I wish I'd had when I first met the Runes. To unite the many interpretations of the Runes, I pulled from a variety of sources, listed on page 99. There turned out to be so much information that I decided to compile it into a workbook. It made the challenge of getting people to experience the Runes for themselves a lot easier. My experience has been that no one actually *teaches* Rune divination to you; it is learned intuitively by playing with them yourself or along with others. It worked. Within a couple of hours people who had never seen a Rune were doing sophisticated readings for each other. I was encouraged to turn the workbook into a 'real' book, and here we are.

I am not a Rune scholar. There are enough of those to argue about all aspects of the Runes. What I know is that they are ancient. The first historically documented use of Runes in a systematic way (as words) is 50 C.E. How long were these symbols in use before then? It's beyond our comprehension. They are an intricate part of our history, perhaps even part of our DNA because of the ease in which people acclimate to them. We have an instinctual knowing as to how they apply or give insight to our lives that just needs to be awakened. That is the intent of this workbook.

The word Rune is found in most Germanic and Celtic languages to mean *mystery* or *secret*. As with the tarot, there is a lot of disagreement over the meanings, where they originated and to what they are associated. I've included all of the associations from different sources, even when they appear to contradict each other. For instance, the colors white *and* black may be listed as the color for the same Rune. This is not a problem for me as I believe that truth exists in paradox. These inconsistencies simply give us a peek into the *mystery* by revealing the range of possibilities in each interpretation. Try to embrace instead of fight it and the doorway to the information will open.

This workbook has: The instructions for making Runes; a few ways to read, remember and translate them; rituals to use; and a list of books that I found helpful. I have outlined each Rune the same way (described below) to give a broad body of information to spark meanings that speak to you.

Order of the Runes: The **Germanic names** sometimes called the Elder Futhark are in bold and the Anglo-Saxon names in ( ). They are placed in the *most* agreed upon 'traditional' order. The name Futhark is the phonetic equivalent that comes from the first six Runes of Freyr, (th is one Rune, *Thurisaz*). This Germanic order comes from the three Norse gods Freyr, Hagel and Tyr, each having 8 Runes. These three groups are known as the *aettir*. The gods are listed in order. If you want to know which Runes belong to whom, start from the beginning and count to eight three times. I have also included the controversial blank Rune, which you can choose to use if you like.

Meanings section: When you read the first line that says *meaning*, understand that this is like looking up a word in the dictionary. We have many words in our language that are used in different ways. So do the Runes. We have many words that have changed meaning over time; for instance 'cool' doesn't just mean 'a bit cold' anymore. The Runes have morphed as well. There is no evidence of the original meanings, but there is poetry and ruins from the 1st century that give us an idea. The most important thing is to think of the meanings visually and in *all* the ways you can think of. Take the ox Rune. Does it feel powerful or like a beast of burden? How do those feeling images apply to you? What jobs do oxen do or have they done? Where are they located in the world? Think with a wide perspective and see which resonates with what you are feeling.

Nature, Healing properties, Think about, Reversed and Represents sections: The information here is varied since it came from many sources. The Runes are multidimensional and can be viewed from many directions; the variety here is to give you a taste of their range. Use what feels most accurate for your situation. If you are pulled to a definition that doesn't make sense, it may be your intuition speaking. Record it and see what happens over time that may bring light to it.

Letter section: This is the letter(s) the Rune is associated with in modern English.

Sound energy section: Playing with these sounds will give you a sensation of the energy and vibration of the Rune. This is fun! And will remind you that a Rune is more than an intellectual exercise.

Number, Element, Color, Stone, Trees, Tarot association sections: These are included to help you cross reference the information you get. If you are more familiar with some of these systems, use and include them with your Rune divinations; they can expand your understanding.

Physical, Emotional, Mental, and Spiritual sections: These help you start thinking of the Runes as a force of energy that can apply to our many dimensions. See if the descriptions feel accurate for you; if not, jot down your own feelings to observe if and/or how they change over time.

Magickal applications: I have spelled magick with a 'k' because it is the traditional way to differentiate between Divine or ritual Magick from slight-of-hand. I have also capitalized it to set it apart as a helpful energy. Many people associate Runes with Magick and ritual. This frightens some and intrigues others. I've included this section to demystify and normalize Magick by showing the everyday applications of Runes. For example, they can be used simply by carrying one in your pocket, drawing it with your finger in the air or making an object such as jewelry to wear. This is simple Magick; there are many books if you want to learn more. Try it yourself and see what works for you.

Body posture (stadha) section: You can feel the physicality and energy focus by moving your body so it takes the shape of a Rune. Try it, it's fun and simple.

Notes section: This book is just a start for you to make your own book to assist you in deciphering the Runes. There is space in every section for you to add your own discoveries. By doing so, you will learn a lot and find it is more meaningful.

I also encourage you to do your own research. The meanings of the Runes come from an oral tradition that has many myths, legends and folklore associated with each one. The stories are rich with symbolic meaning, memorable and entertaining to read. The tales help breathe new meaning into each Rune. I have not included stories with each Rune because others do this much better. I particularly love *The Woman's Book of Runes* by Susan Gray. She gives short synopses of a wealth of stories that are linked to history and tradition. They are delightful to read and tie together everything in a quick understandable bundle.

I have compiled bits and pieces of information for you to think about. But the source I encourage the most is from the place of inner knowing. Scholars might be horrified by this, but this is a way I believe Runes can be used by everyone. They are a way to open our intuition so we can *feel* what is right for us in the moment. Anyone who does divinations knows that the same set of cards or coins or yarrow sticks can be pulled/thrown a different day and have a totally different meaning. These tools give us a different perspective on life, ultimately allowing us to make more informed choices.

Most of this book was written in 2009, which is considered a mineral year in the tradition of the Dagara tribe of Burkina Faso, Africa. A mineral year is a time where there are strong energies present to help us with communication. I like to think those energies helped me write about this ancient form of deep communication. My hope is that it wakes up your dormant knowing of the Runes and brings perspective, joy and magick to your life.

Jennifer Halls, January 2011
Fort Mill, South Carolina

How to Use this Book

#1 Have fun! I planned to make the subtitle of this book *playbook* instead of *workbook* but it just seemed too flakey. Yet that's what this is - suggestions for a way to play while developing your intuitive awareness. A curious, open mind in a relaxed setting is the perfect environment for cultivating self-knowledge and intuitive wisdom. Bending over a book with your brows furrowed and doing exercises you hate is not. So if there is something you don't want to do in this book, don't do it. If you read something and think of a better way to experience it, do it. This book is yours; now make it your own. I wrote the perfect book for my Runes experience in hopes of inspiring others to have their perfect experience. What works for me may not for you. Use this workbook as a loose guide to begin *your* Rune play.

#2 Get some Runes! Better still, make your own set. If you have a set you want to use, use them. You can make a set in 5 minutes with paper pieces and a pen, or get ideas for fancier materials on page 67. You can create a ritual from page 69, or not. There is a lot to choose from. Remember, the energy of joy in any creative act imbues whatever you are making with a powerful Magick. Enjoy!

And/or: Use the meanings in this book with the set of Runes you make and do simple readings

Or/and: Purchase or borrow as many books on Runes as you can to collect the stories and different uses. The books listed in the back are excellent. Take the first Rune and go from book to book, making notes in the space provided. This gives you a more spherical view of the Rune and its many meanings. Do this with each Rune and Magick automatically happen. This will help your mind rest so your intuition can make its way to the forefront. You won't need to remember, don't try to; you can always reference your notes. You automatically will begin to connect to something bigger – your intuition. You will be amazed by the results. *(This can also be done by looking up Rune sites and meanings on the internet.)*

And/or: Find a friend(s) to do this with. Each of you will take a Rune to research and then come back and tell stories about them to each other. The Runes are a part of an oral tradition based around folklore/myths/legends that convey wisdom through stories. One of the best ways to learn them is to be entertained while gaining their wisdom and meaning. Write poems, do plays, sing songs, tell jokes, etc. Let yourself be inspired to convey meanings in a new way. Learn, teach and have fun, all at the same time.

Or/ and: Forget the whole set, just learn to write your name and discover its meaning with the exercises in the back.

And/or: Do whatever you want; your mind is now oiled to come up with your own ideas.

The Runes...

Fehu (Feoh)   *pronounced 'FAY-hu'*

Meaning: cattle/wealth (cattle was a type of currency in ancient times)
Nature: feminine
Number: 1
Healing properties: honesty, be true to yourself
Element: fire/earth
Letter: F
Sound energy: fffff – like crackling fire or hissing
Color: red/gold
Stone: carnelian, green tourmaline, amber
Trees: birch, alder, flax
Tarot association: High priestess, Tower
Physical: money, wealth; sexual passion
Emotional: sense of self worth
Mental: ego, how you focus the mind positively or negatively
Spiritual: karma- law of cause and effect

Think about: profit and gain coming into your life; fertility; conserving what has been gained; sharing; mindfulness of how you use power; personal reserves; ambition satisfied; rewards received. Where do I get true nourishment?

Reversed - think about: reckless behavior; misuse of wealth or power; greed/envy; burden from too much; monitoring resources going out; failure/getting it wrong; bankrupt; loss of self esteem; contraction/restriction. Are you hiding your light?

Magickal applications: inner power; for attracting wealth and protecting property; gives you a larger capacity to send and receive energies whether good or bad.

Body posture (stadha): Stand with both arms slanting up and to the left, the left arm being a bit higher. Facing toward the sun your fingers are pointed to direct the energy; palms are up to draw in force.

Fehu represents:

- moveable wealth, possessions and responsibility of using it as a positive force
- circulating abundance
- prophecy and gifts of knowledge, the power to divine
- source energy and that which sustains life
- primordial fire, creative source
- archetypal energy of motion and expansion
- creation/destruction

Notes:

One word that sums up this Rune for me is

Uruz (Ur)   *pronounced 'OO-rooz'*

Meaning: aurochs (the power of wild cattle/ox)
Nature: masculine
Number: 2
Healing properties: feeling grateful (great-full), appreciation
Element: earth
Letter: U
Sound energy: uuu - like the 'oo' in noon, long and force-filled like the ox
Color: green-brown
Stone: tiger eye, hawk eye
Trees: oak
Tarot association: Tower, High Priestess, Hierophant
Physical: strength and flexibility in healing
Emotional: strength and balance
Mental: using the will wisely
Spiritual: internal transition; spiritual fortitude

Think about: a healing force at work within you; how to build strength and release weakness; positive changes; effort and will with focus shape your circumstances; good fortune; vitality and health; release to birth anew; harnessing wild energy to manifest and build. Has a strong virile male entered your life? Can you make time to center and focus wisely?

Reversed - think about: an obstacle may be in your way; difficulties with sex; health problems; failing to take action in an important moment; lack of will power; changes taking place may not be for the best; missed chances; minor illness; bad luck. Are you willing to take care of yourself?

Magickal applications: enhances groundedness & strength; removes self doubt; use to start a new process; divert difficulties through sudden change; weaken an enemy or judgment; draw on your forehead for energy.

Body posture (stadha): Stand facing east. Bend over at the waist with your back straight until horizontal and parallel to the floor. Point the fingers and arms toward the ground with your eyes facing the floor.

Uruz represents:

- enduring strength, physical power and activity
- maintaining health on every level
- life force drawn from the earth for bold action
- helps with change, movement and overcoming obstacles
- challenges appear for growth
- channeling wild, aggressive energy into trained warrior
- in order to rule you must learn how to serve
- must tear down to build anew
- invitation to count your blessings, find beauty

Notes:

One word that sums up this Rune for me is

Thuisaz (Thorn) *pronounced 'THUR-ee-sahz'*

Meaning: giant; originally meant 'the good one' was later made evil
Nature: masculine
Number: 3
Healing properties: the love and understanding gained through wisdom heals all
Element: fire
Letter: TH
Sound energy: thu – grunt like a giant, loud & forceful, repeating & each ending abruptly
Color: bright red
Stone: agate, bloodstone, hematite
Trees: hawthorn, oak, houseleek
Tarot association: Emperor
Physical: protection; unfortunate event; small irritations that are manageable
Emotional: breakthrough- allow uncomfortable emotions help recognize what's needed
Mental: self-discipline, organization
Spiritual: purification; divine opening

Think about: a force of awakening and growth; pregnant with possibilities and break-through is now possible; stop dealing with others small irritating problems; having unrelenting strength; drawing on blessings and protection from the divine; give thoughtful time and enlist second opinions to important decisions for they will change your direction; move away from negative energies. What part of your life needs a lighting bolt to break through old patterns or to illuminate? What needs to be cleansed by fire so it can regenerate?

Reversed - think about: in general it's a warning to stay present and be careful when making choices; progress may be restricted or blocked; unwilling to seek advice from others; stuck in a blind spot; you need to get grounded and release frustration. Where are you blocked or held in old patterns? Are you being stubborn about 'doing it yourself'? Who can you call on for help? If you can think of no one, call on the Divine to guide your way.

Magickal applications: use care as it brings a catalyst for change, regeneration, beginnings and for defense and protection; thunderbolts can be cast to break obstructions and bring about new beginnings.

Body posture (stadha): Face east or south and stand straight with your left arm bent with the palm of your left hand holding your hip (like posing for the 'I'm a little teapot' song). Right arm is down to the side, fingers straight and palm on side of leg.

Thuisaz represents:

- obstacles revealed
- divine protection and human defense
- mental blocks and the shadow side

Notes:

One word that sums up this Rune for me is

Ansuz (Os)   *pronounced 'AHN-sooz'*

Meaning: a god, mouth, the primal sound, oaum
Nature: masculine trio (father, son and Sage)
Number: 4
Healing properties: self honesty, amends and restoration of faith on all levels
Element: air
Letter: A
Sound energy: ah or aaaaaa – like the 'a' in all
Color: dark blue
Stone: lapis lazuli
Trees: ash, hazel
Tarot association: Death, Hermit, Hierophant, Fool
Physical: leadership inside and out
Emotional: overcoming fear
Mental: conscious planning and thinking
Spiritual: access to divine wisdom

Think about: contacting a living person who gives wise counsel; your vision is truest when it comes from a deep source; listen closely within you; listen closely to those around you for useful information; increasing powers of self expression will bring clarity; using your voice in incantations as a container and an expresser of a magical force; use persuasive speech to gain advantage. Is there a teacher, scholar, counselor or elder you need to study with? Is what's coming out of your mouth what you mean to say?

Reversed - think about: be on guard against tricksters, smooth talkers, bad advice or get rich quick schemes; boredom, frustration or the mundane is affecting you and your choices; chaos makes it hard to discern fact from fiction. Do you have hidden agendas? Where is poor communication affecting you? Are you lying to yourself or others, or are you being lied to? Where are you ignorant or lacking inspiration?

Magickal applications: increases the power of: words, inspiration and intuitive skills; brings light and promotes calm presence; can help release binding situations/vows; this is Odin's Rune (a god credited with designing the Runes) - invoke his wisdom/inspiration.

Body posture (stadha): Standing straight face north or east. Put both arms out parallel to the ground palms down, then bring the arms down so they mirror the angle of the Rune, with the left arm lower than the right. Palms are facing down.

Ansuz Represents:

- effective speech, listening and overall communication
- bringing the unconscious into consciousness
- releasing restrictions so wisdom can be received
- helps give expression to inner wisdom to release confusion and illusion
- sacred stories and songs of our history- the Rune for artists, writers & storytellers.
- the power of naming and of rewriting the stories you tell yourself

Notes:

One word that sums up this Rune for me is

Raidho (Rad) *pronounced 'Rah-EED-ho'*

Meaning: riding, wheel, vehicle, journey action
Nature: masculine
Number: 5
Healing properties: surrendering, letting go to allow Divine help in
Element: air
Letter: R
Sound energy: rrrrrrr - a rolled r, like a Scottish burr or a boat motor starting
Color: bright red
Stone: turquoise
Trees: holly, oak
Tarot association: Chariot, Wheel of fortune, Hierophant, Sun
Physical: travel, take a trip, holiday pleasure
Emotional: honesty, with feelings to get on course
Mental: allowing a different perspective to change thought patterns
Spiritual: a turn onto or opening of a soul path

Think about: daily path guided by the sun; independent travel or journey physically and spiritually; indicates moving and evolving in harmony; the journey outside is always the journey inside; ordering your life to the greatest benefit or economical use of energy; ability to find your own rhythm and timing to effortlessly make progress in life; knowing yourself and being in sync with your intuition; accepting responsibility and focus. Have you asked your body, your knowing, and your spirit through prayer about right action to take? Do you trust your process or are you 'trying' to make it happen?

Reversed - think about: aimless wandering instead of real progress; blaming others; error in judgment, just say no; double check reservations and car maintenance; failure to pay attention to detail resulting in errors and disorder; roadblocks and failures may be rerouting something for you. Are you willing to make the effort to experience something new? Are you watching the world pass you by?

Magickal applications: use for safe travel; use it to reinforce the pattern of spells to bind them to work in the natural pattern of the universe; can move or remove energies and direct them to a specific destination; can be used as a guide into trance.

Body posture (stadha): Stand straight facing south. Put your elbow out by putting your left palm on your left hip joint. Your right arm is straight down hugged to your side. Put your left leg slanted out like the Rune slightly lifted off of the ground.

Raidho represents:

- putting events in a larger perspective
- travel to broaden the mind and change how we see things
- cycles of time, rites of passage, the patterns beneath all life as shown by time
- the straight path, the 'right way' to live in alignment with the cosmos
- labyrinth wheel, going between worlds where all life/death/rebirth is perceivable

Notes:

One word that sums up this Rune for me is

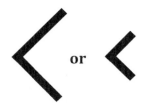 or

Kenaz (Cen)   *pronounced 'KEN-ahz'*

Meaning: torch, a beacon
Nature: feminine
Number: 6
Healing properties: peace stemming from the place of deep self acceptance
Element: fire
Letter: K or Q
Sound energy: keh – a loud hard K sound that tapers down, softening on the breath
Color: light red, orange
Stone: flint, smoky quartz, fire-agate, amber
Trees: pine, maidenhair
Tarot association: Chariot, Wheel of Fortune, Moon
Physical: conception of a child; the many ways of creating
Emotional: enthusiasm, joy; peace
Mental: success; solutions, clarity
Spiritual: illumination, enlightenment

Think about: overwhelming urge to create or bring new energy to something; an opening is here for you to easily go though; you are in touch with the power to create your own reality; look at how you are using your energy (life force); the importance of controlled fire (energy); passion and lust; kindling of knowledge within, knowing of hidden matters; to stoke this flame brings change on every level. What do you have enthusiasm and passion for? Do you give yourself time to spend with spiritual guidance?

Reversed - think about: loss; choosing to look at the darkness (negativity) instead of the light; restriction self imposed or closed off; lack of control; blocks in the way of transformation and change; imbalanced sexual life could be sterile or barren; unhealed trauma. Are you letting others control your life? Are you using drugs or alcohol to block your senses?

Magickal applications: call on this ever-burning flame to manifest your needs and desires; to strengthen; for love and stability in relationships; fresh starts; physical healing; can banish unwanted influences be it inner or outer; can be used for protection of valuables; increases artistic craft, mental agility and spiritual communication.

Body posture (stadha): Stand straight and raise your right arm to a 45° angle, palm down to draw in energy. Continue by lowering the left arm by the same angle as the Rune, palm is down and fingers are pointed to project and manifest the energy.

Kenaz represents:

- the inner light of deep knowing
- connection with spiritual guidance
- clarity and insight and opening
- change, birth
- opposites bound together to become manifest
- teaching and learning

Notes:

One word that sums up this Rune for me is _____

Gebo (Gifu)   *pronounced 'GHEB-o'*

Meaning: gift, a sacred mark, a gift to the gods
Nature: feminine
Number: 7
Healing properties: the courage it takes to be trusting
Element: air
Letter: G
Sound energy: geh – like the 'g' in getup, repeat evenly and cyclically
Color: deep blue, emerald green
Stone: emerald, jade
Trees: ash, elm, apple
Tarot association: Lovers, High Priestess
Physical: opportunity; material gift; a relationship becomes more permanent
Emotional: ecstasy and peace
Mental: generous attitude
Spiritual: divine gift or skill; vow

Think about: a time of prosperity, peace, overall good fortune; recognize the gifts you have given, received or exchanged; joined forces like a wedding or contract; all gifts are an energy exchange - be conscious of what you give and receive; male/female polarity; an offering to the divine; two way exchange increases the power of both parties. Who can you physically or psychically join with to create a mutual positive affect greater than the whole? Do you receive as well as you give?

There is no Reversed position. Think about what's hidden, unconscious or what other Runes surround it: miserly spirit; wasted gifts; unable to appreciate; unequal exchange; greed; arguments; being taken advantage of; loosing or fearing to speak up about being slighted. Have you collapsed into or lost yourself in a relationship? Are you taking advantage or being taken advantage of? Are you giving pearls to swine?

Magickal applications: use to help recognize and actualize your own gifts; call on to help your inner power bring forth something; sexual magic and mystical unions; luck, crossing the fingers invokes this Rune; enhances marriages, partnership, contracts of mutual agreement.

Body posture (stadha): Stand with your legs wide apart, feet forward and knees locked. Stretch your arms up and directly over your feet so your body is a big X.

Gebo represents:

- giving and receiving
- the law of cause and effect
- partnership where the individuals remain whole
- inner gifts and giving of the self

Notes:

One word that sums up this Rune for me is

Wunjo (Wyn) *pronounced 'WOON-yo'*

Meaning: joy, perfection
Nature: masculine
Number: 8
Healing properties: allowing, opening to a serene presence
Element: earth
Letter: W or V
Sound energy: wwwwww – like the 'w' in when, a deep buzzing w sound
Color: purple, green, yellow
Stone: topaz, rose quartz
Trees: ash, bramble, ivy
Tarot association: Strength, Hierophant
Physical: celebration; great conversations
Emotional: joy, happiness in the fullness of life
Mental: confidence and success
Spiritual: harmony and fulfillment

Think about: good news that makes life better; this is the energy that binds different fields of force together; harmoniously working with others; wishes fulfilled; unity with a common desire, standard or goal; positive use of your will. Are you allowing yourself to feel content? Are you enjoying the company of others?

Reversed - think about: lacking confidence; seemingly insurmountable problems; depression or feelings that people don't care for you; tension, unhappiness or disharmony in the family or group; a weakening friendship; aggressive behavior. Are you viewing things pessimistically? Are you 'acting' like a know it all?

Magickal applications: use it as the final significator for the success and happiness of magic created; help to relieve stress; brings contact with like minded people.

Body posture (stadha): Stand straight with your right arm down, close to your side and your legs together. Place just the fingers of your left hand on top of your head, with your elbow out to your left side to look like this Rune.

Wunjo represents:

- harmony with the flow of events
- a wish coming true
- being bound with friends though pleasure and fellowship
- natural contentment

Notes:

One word that sums up this Rune for me is _____

Hagalaz (haegl) *pronounced 'HA-ga-lahz'*
Note - this Rune has two ways that it can appear

Meaning: hail; transformation; two beams connected or two realms connected
Nature: feminine (triple goddess)
Number: 9
Healing properties: allowing anger to be your friend and using it appropriately
Element: ice
Letter: H
Sound energy: hhhhhh - a forceful long exhale
Color: light blue
Stone: crystal, jet
Trees: ash, yew, elder, nightshade
Tarot association: World, Devil, Emperor
Physical: disruption, chaotic change unable to control
Emotional: anger, angst
Mental: disillusionment
Spiritual: dark night of the soul; general struggle

Think about: can be a fore-warning of unpleasant events or upset of plans; the saying - 'God is hitting you over the head with a brick to get your attention'; lay low for awhile and meditate on the issues around you; everything taken for granted is challenged; the more severe the disruption the more the more significant your growth; seeing delays in a positive way by recognizing them as part of the natural order or pattern of things; what's bad is good and reasons will be seen at a later date; being swept along spiritually by forces beyond your control; Goddess as destroyer, protector and Creatrix. Where are you too comfortable in life? Can you appreciate the small stuff during difficult times?

There is no Reversed position. Think about what's hidden, unconscious or what other Runes surround it: be cautious when making long term plans; what looks to be bad is really about change and growth for the better; disasters caused by natural forces; delays or circumstances beyond individual control. Are you jumping into things too quickly? Are you looking at challenges negatively?

Magickal applications: its use in Magick is different than in divination, use this to secure a slow, steady evolution within a fixed framework; it has a fixed nature that secures a space and keeps it safely from negative energies; bring unity into your life with this controller and focuser of energies; use to attract positive influences.

Body posture (stadha): Stand straight with both arms stretched out to your sides, even with your shoulders and parallel to the ground. Palms face up.

Hagalaz represents:

- disruption, disorientation, chaos
- frustrating delays, slow movement
- passage between the two worlds
- the great awakener, the Mother Rune

Notes:

One word that sums up this Rune for me is

Naudhiz (Nyd)   *pronounced* 'NOWD-heez'

Meaning: need, necessity
Nature: feminine
Number: 10
Healing properties: the transformation of being ashamed into powerful self-knowledge
Element: fire
Letter: N
Sound energy: n - pronounce the letter 'n' exploring different ways to feel and say it
Color: black
Stone: obsidian
Trees: beech, rowan, alder
Tarot association: The Devil, Tower, Death
Physical: need for material things
Emotional: need for emotional comfort
Mental: need for wisdom
Spiritual: need for spiritual solace

Think about: blocks/restrictions that lead to self-knowing; the point in your cycle when you are ready for change; pay off debts; mend what needs to be repaired; setbacks are coming, so focus on finishing before proceeding; long lasting success for choices made with careful consideration; the primal need that makes you seek a mate/lover; using your will you can create magic; owning your divine spark; know there are many ways to do things; valuable time and energy can be wasted if not intuitively attuned. Are you able to accept your fate? Can you develop patience? Can you draw from your hidden potential? Are you relaxing and playing enough?

Reversed - think about: forewarns of failure; may be in a situation that seems hopeless to escape from; getting what's needed instead of what's wanted; examine your motives before proceeding; rash action can lead to failure; better to reconsider or cancel rather than to hastily move forward; stress related problems; restrain impulses, control anger, seek faith; odds feel stacked against you. Are you resistant to another way of doing things? Is greed clouding your vision? Have you disowned a part of yourself?

Magickal applications: overcoming distress; help with finding a lover; to help lost causes; for the development of Magickal will and spiritual power; spiritual protection; used to banish the negative to bring in the positive; cast with love it will bring strength to those who need it; use for freeing the real self.

Body posture (stadha): Face south. Stand straight with the right arm up to the side palm up, the same angle as the Rune, and the left arm, palm down, slanting down to form a straight line with the right arm.

Naudhiz represents:

- need, distress, pain and the release from it
- need-fire created by friction and resistance calls will directed action
- forces of destiny are working so use caution, resist greed
- bringing light to the shadow
- no pain, no gain

Notes:

One word that sums up this Rune for me is

Isa (Is) *pronounced 'EE-sa'*

Meaning: ice, icicle, inertia
Nature: feminine
Number: 11
Healing properties: the transformative power of recognizing what we are afraid of
Element: ice
Letters: I or J
Sound energy: eecceecc – a high pitched, sharp continuous sound
Color: white, black
Stone: diamond
Trees: blackthorn, alder, beech
Tarot association: Hanged Man, Hermit, Justice
Physical: stop and slow down
Emotional: peace, calm
Mental: stillness
Spiritual: inactivity

Think about: winter; standstill or gestation time that precedes a rebirth; plans are on hold and no activity is useful; wait until you have real energy to proceed with a project; cooling off time in a romantic relationship - may need time apart or space to know what's desired; discord with friends; a time to cultivate inner will and control; if it appears and is surrounded by Runes signifying difficulties you may not want to proceed with the event, project or relationship; a strong will can overcome any negative situation. Do you allow yourself to take time to enjoy times of rest and non-action? Do you allow yourself enough time to sit with a situation that needs resolution? Can you be neutral?

There is no Reversed position. Think about what's hidden, unconscious or what other Runes surround it: Are you too introspective, lazy or selfish? Have you been behaving carelessly? Are you spacing out to escape life? Has your heart turned to stone? Are you depressed?

Magickal applications: to ground and calm a situation or chaotic emotions; to freeze a condition to stay as it is; to block, slow or stop unwanted forces or events; help with concentration and inner focus; to shield or cancel unwanted aggressiveness, arguments or harassments.

Body posture (stadha): Either stand straight with your arms against your sides OR stand straight with your arms overhead, palms together, fingers pointing up.

Isa represents:

- stillness and waiting, patience
- lack of vibration, a black hole
- neutrality
- ego
- bridge for over the waters and between the worlds
- spiritual blind-spot

Notes:

One word that sums up this Rune for me is

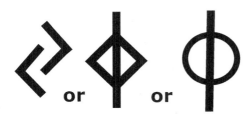

Jera (Ger)   *pronounced 'YARE-a'*
Note - this Rune has three ways that it can appear

Meaning: year, harvest
Nature: feminine
Number: 12
Healing properties: Being patient
Element: earth
Letter: J or Y
Sound energy: y – simple short sound like the 'y' in year, play with the sound/feel of it
Color: light blue, red, green
Stone: moss agate
Trees: oak
Tarot association: Fool, Justice
Physical: improvement in the material realm; new job or relationship; birth
Emotional: recouping your energy to feel more in-tune
Mental: better outlook on life
Spiritual: forward movement with a spiritual quest or attainment

Think about: long term improvement toward change for the better; debts will be repaid; conception and/or birth; rewards arriving at the 'right' time; rewards from any endeavor that you are committed to; yearly cyclical path guided by the sun; continue to persevere; patience with yourself and your process; by judging others, you will be judged; harsh words or actions will end things, a friendship, business, etc.; natural justice/cosmic order; fruition; remember there are cycles to everything. Are you forcing things by thinking to linearly? Are you working in harmony? Do you remember that everything has a cycle?

There is no Reversed position. Think about what's hidden, unconscious or what other Runes surround it: don't try to force a birth before it's time; poor results are coming from the work done without proper groundwork; being unfairly judged; inability to work with the natural cycles of things; disappointments; miscarriage, divorce or lost lawsuit. Are you being careless with how you approach things? Have you asked yourself if it's really the right time to start something? Do you need to develop patience?

Magickal applications: helps in legal matters; helps bring the true material results from time, money or effort given; brings the culmination of events or processes; fertility; joyous laughter helps to call forth the blessings of this Rune.

Body posture (stadha): Stand straight and bring your right arm straight out in front of you; bend it so that the right thumb and forefinger touch the crown of the head. Bring your left arm straight behind you; bend it down so that your fingertips touch the left hip.

Jera represents:

- end of a cycle and beginning a different one
- positive return on one's actions
- a blessing on the work you have begun
- fertility, creativity
- one year cycle, a 12 fold rotation
- reaping what you sow, karma

Notes:

One word that sums up this Rune for me is

Eihwaz (Eoh)   *pronounced 'EYE-warz'*

Meaning: yew tree, regeneration, longevity
Nature: masculine
Number: 13
Healing properties: accepting the truth, conscious living
Element: all water, earth, air, fire, ice
Letters: E or I
Sound energy: ei – like the 'i' in stride, intone evenly and powerfully from the diaphragm
Color: dark blue, dark green
Stone: smoky quartz
Trees: yew, hemlock, beech
Tarot association: Hangman, Death, Chariot, Devil
Physical: old friend/enemy contacts; a death; unexpected change move for the better
Emotional: owning what we have disowned
Mental: facing our inner demons
Spiritual: initiation; release from the fear of death

Think about: patience; do not act, the delay is beneficial before action is taken.; a person or spirit 'shows up' from your past; difficulties are normal at the beginning of something new, use perseverance; a trying, yet meaningful time currently or ahead; a death; see the consequences before you act; a clearing of old energies so a situation can rest; enduring a painful ordeal that helps you gain inner wisdom; protection provided for the difficult trials of life. Do you have a clear aim for or view of your goal? What kind of initiation are you going through? Do you need to clear some clutter out of your life/office/home?

There is no Reversed position. Think about what's hidden, unconscious or what other Runes surround it: giving up too soon; being too fixed and inflexible to navigate to the end; weak willed, unable to see things through; recurrence of old problems; self-delusion; false recollections of and over dwelling on the 'good old days'; accidental or disease related death of a loved one; being witness to or participating in addiction or path of destruction. What do you need to set your home or business in order? What are you obsessing on that isn't healthy? Where are you being lazy?

Magickal applications: ends situations; solves problems; gives strength, courage and endurance; protection from ghosts; removes obstacles; increases power; finding true aim of focus; use as a guard against self destructive behavior/addiction; use to find a job, home or something lost; do not use negatively it can bring death and reek havoc; deflects and prevents.

Body posture (stadha): Stand straight and reach both arms together (palms down) out in front of you. Then move them down to mimic the top angle of the Rune. Now lift either your right or left foot to the parallel angle in the back.

Eihwaz represents:

- lasting flexibility, strength and consciousness
- altered consciousness
- connection to/communication with heaven, earth and the underworld
- unifying life and death
- initiation

Notes:

One word that sums up this Rune for me is

Perthro (Peorth)   *pronounced* 'PER-thro'

Meaning: cup for throwing lots
Nature: feminine
Number: 14
Healing properties: the warm radiating Love that comes from the Divine
Element: water
Letter: P
Sound energy: peh – a full rounded deep sound
Color: black, dark purple, red, white (the Norn's colors)
Stone: onyx
Trees: beech, yew, elder
Tarot association: Wheel of Fortune, Tower
Physical: real magick; secrets uncovered; a positive surprise
Emotional: trusting/resting in the fates
Mental: interest in the occult
Spiritual: divine guidance and help

Think about: the knowing that you're not supposed to know; your past actions and the way you respond to things is what creates your future; go out and dance or sing; small actions sent and received, the 'butterfly effect'; a spiritual guide points the way; people will offer help; hidden knowledge revealed; unexpected gains; help arrives that may not be recognized until much later. Are you ready to shed your old skin? What is the external reflecting about your internal state? Are you open to receive help?

Reversed - think about: negative; bad luck; beware of making rash or stupid moves right now; unseen things working against you; don't take any chances right now - don't gamble, loan money, tell secrets; don't buy costly items like cars or property, things are not as they seem; things you want to hide (scandals, embarrassments, indiscretions, skeletons) will be revealed; repeating old patterns causes suffering; overwhelm and exhaustion with life's challenges. Are you taking enough time before you act? Are you healing addictions?

Magickal applications: allied with karmic energies, it helps find things hidden or lost; use when dealing with investments or finances; use for good mental health and healing; use to obtain wise inner guidance and to help find your path; for understanding past incarnations and ancestral memories; use for divination; for investment information.

Body posture (stadha): Sit on the ground facing west with your knees together and bent, feet on the ground and back straight. Bring your elbows together to rest on your knees.

Move your forearms out mirroring the same angle as your calves, then face your palms up so they are out over your feet.

Perthro represents:

- the act of divination
- womb, birth, initiation
- fate or destiny
- hidden talents, inner potential, secrets
- constant change that always remains the same
- the collective unconscious

Notes:

One word that sums up this Rune for me is

Elhaz (Eolh)   *pronounced 'EL-hazh'*

Meaning: elk, totem provides protection
Nature: masculine
Number: 15
Healing properties: the ability to say 'no' and make conscious choices
Element: air
Letter: Z or S
Sound energy: zzzzzz – a buzzing z, like the 's' in cousin
Color: gold, silver-blue
Stone: black tourmaline
Trees: yew, rowan
Tarot association: Moon, Lovers
Physical: outside help and assistance; possible mentor
Emotional: safe, healthy and balanced; clear boundaries
Mental: confidence from having secure ethics
Spiritual: divine protection and connection

Think about: new friendships; positive influences coming into life; deflecting hostility, aggression or annoyances, literally 'talk to the hand'; new lucrative career possibilities; an expansive time where the sky is the limit; senses can be enhanced, psychic episodes; your guardian angel is active. Can you proceed with confidence knowing you are protected? What do you need to do to make your boundaries healthy and clear?

Reversed - think about: negative or dangerous; immunity is down; be aware of your health; be conscious of who you are associating with; material loss; being mislead or misleading people; beware of being dishonest or dishonesty in others; temptation and vulnerability; paranoia and/or over-protectiveness can be making matters worse. Are you being honest with yourself? Can you take a break and lay low for awhile?

Magickal applications: protection from and banishment of negativity, evil and enemies; drawing down energy from the heavens; strengthens bonds for friendships, life force and luck; can increase one's magickal power; draw with your finger in the air around anything you want to protect.

Body posture (stadha): Stand straight with your arms up and out to the sides. Notice the difference when the palms down as apposed to up, both ways work. Feel what's appropriate for your intent.

Elhaz represents:

- protection and defense, a splayed hand
- movement of energies, renewing and regenerative
- the continuance of life
- protection of and from family friends and community
- victory
- sanctuary

Notes:

One word that sums up this Rune for me is

ϟ or **Ϟ**

Sowilo (Sigil) *pronounced 'So-WEE-lo*
Note - this Rune has two ways that it can appear

Meaning: sun, guiding light by land or sea
Nature: feminine
Number: 16
Healing properties: seeing yourself and others through the eyes of compassion
Element: air
Letter: S
Sound energy: sssssssss – with force through the teeth or soft like a snake
Color: white, golden-white
Stone: sun stone
Trees: juniper
Tarot association: Sun, Temperance, Judgment
Physical: success; healing and direction; joyous dance
Emotional: happiness and laughter
Mental: clarity and achievement
Spiritual: unity with the divine

Think about: your connection to spiritual forces; divine help following the soul's path and the realization of your true life direction; it is time to walk away from pain and unhappiness; become conscious of your essence, you have everything you need; you're your own rebirth; what you are striving to become you already are; healing strength is increased; ascending from a spiritual plateau; the blinding light of justice comes through. Are you oriented to your inner/soul compass? Are you letting help from spirit channel through you? Do you recognize your own light and smile?

There is no Reversed position. Think about what's hidden, unconscious or what other Runes surround it: if in an isolated position, indicates health problems; you're in a blind spot; warns against over-doing, unhealthy eating, constant stress, will lead to loss of life force and illness; time for recharging at a core level; illumination, allowing 'right' action to flow through you. Are you being a control freak? If you have so many things going on at once that nothing is done well, what can you let go of?

Magickal applications: use when strength and self confidence are needed; for success; increase sexual power and health; use for spiritual direction; great to use for healing on any level as it brings light/life force; allows one to shield or strike at will; use this pure light in difficult times; it is only helpful energy.

Body posture (stadha): stand and let your body form to the shape of an S. Keep your legs together and arms at your sides; bend your knees and then lean forward a bit.

Sowilo represents:

- victory of the use of the spiritual will and intent
- success or triumph over darkness
- light, spiritual guidance or force that drives us on our path
- ever rotating life giving energy of the universe

Notes:

One word that sums up this Rune for me is

Tiewaz (TYR)   *pronounced 'TEE-wahz'*

Meaning: warrior, sky, justice
Nature: masculine
Number: 17
Healing properties: acting even though you are afraid, courage
Element: air
Letter: T
Sound energy: tiw - rhymes with two, repeat it in short bursts of sound
Color: bright red, crimson
Stone: bloodstone, hematite
Trees: oak, Holm oak, monkshood
Tarot association: Emperor, Justice, Strength, Star, World
Physical: winning a battle; passionate sex
Emotional: fulfillment
Mental: focus on 'right' action and order
Spiritual: faith and trust

Think about: when we trust in the divine we trust ourselves; to uphold justice, a personal sacrifice may be required; maintain your integrity and ethics and the truth will win; if pulled by a man it represents him; if pulled by a woman it can represent the closest male to her or means a strong male love relationship is on the way; knowing your place in the natural order of things; a good sexual relationship; emotionally fulfilled; success with legal issues; self conquest, a spiritual warrior always battles himself. Are you willing to make a personal sacrifice because it's right? Are you taking responsibility for your actions? Do you trust your intuition to guide you?

Reversed - think about: legal issues; marital problems, end of a relationship, celibacy, one sided love; if pulled by a woman she's having trouble with men in general; if pulled by a man trouble with self image and feeling inadequate; emotional difficulties from past negative experiences; trust issues. Are you trying to control someone else? Are you practicing double standards? Are you perverting the truth, playing unfairly or cheating?

Magickal applications: to overcome adversity; rights things when you have been falsely accused or unfairly treated; for quick recuperation with health issues.

Body posture (stadha): Stand straight, arms are straight down to the sides, now raise them both out about 20 inches, making your body look like an arrow. Feel the difference between the palms facing up or down, use the position that feels closest to your intent.

Tiewaz represents:

- victory, divine justice, honorable warrior's success
- confronting unfairness
- discipline and faith according to divine law
- the 3 fold mystery - justice, war & world-column (this column upholds the whole universe)
- positive form of strong male energy

Notes:

One word that sums up this Rune for me is

Berkana (Beorc)   *pronounced 'BER-kah-no'*

Meaning: birch tree, bride, mother, earth energy for rebirthing
Nature: feminine
Number: 18
Healing properties: praying as a way of being present with the Divine
Element: earth
Letter: B
Sound energy: bbbbbb – an almost closed lipped, deep, soft hum
Color: dark green, white
Stone: amber, jet
Trees: birch
Tarot association: Magician, Empress
Physical: the birth or conception of a job, relationship, child, etc.
Emotional: well-being
Mental: the birth or conception of an idea, goal, dream
Spiritual: intuition

Think about: purify, cleanse and clear a way for what is being born; a fresh beginning to nurture and attend to; marriage or a birth; a 'meeting of the minds'; when a woman pulls this Rune it represents her; when a man pulls this Rune it represents his closest female relationship; passive receptivity opens the flow of energies that bare fruit; sacred sex. Are you enjoying caring for what's new in your life? Do you listen to your gut/ inner voice?

Reversed - think about: things may be in disguise so don't be mislead by the physical appearance; interference and difficulty with starting fresh; an undesirable mother figure or difficulties in the family; not being courageous enough to take the 'right' action; blocks to growth; lack of nurturing, time or being fed. Are you putting your wants above others needs? Are you holding onto what's outdated and needs to go?

Magickal applications: to bring ideas to fruition; fertility; harmony in the household; peace and protection; strengthens, protects and conceals secrets, those that need to hide from danger and those that have just been conceived; helps to contain many energies and unify them; attracts goodness; heals female health issues; for loving energies.

Body posture (stadha): Stand straight with your right arm down against your right side. Lift your left elbow and place your left hand on your hip. Lift your left knee and turn it to the left and rest your foot on your right ankle. The left elbow and knee form the angled B.

Berkana represents:

- the Great Mother, love and nurturing feminine energy, breasts
- rebirth and renewal
- purification, healing and health
- creative power, beauty
- intuition

Notes:

One word that sums up this Rune for me is _____

Ehwaz (Eh)   *pronounced 'EAY-wahz'*

Meaning: horse, an intuitive bond (as with a horse and rider)
Nature: feminine
Number: 19
Healing properties: forgiving yourself and others as a way to cleanse and honor the past
Element: earth
Letter: E
Sound energy: ay – like in play, let the sound be long and drawn out
Color: white, orange-red
Stone: turquoise
Trees: oak, ash, alder, ragwort
Tarot association: Lovers, Chariot, Sun
Physical: positive movement with another; relocation
Emotional: good, open, trusting feelings
Mental: minds are attuned with another
Spiritual: intuition, connection with the divine

Think about: good travel; relocation of home; balanced use of sexual energy; makes just about anything better; sharing good fortune; you are headed in a direction where two parties will reap rewards; maintain trust and harmony with those you are working/living with, the combined effort moves you forward; momentum with regard to change. Are you ready to share the reins of your life? Can you open to intimacy with joy?

Reversed - think about: action, movement and opportunities are blocked; warning that travel may be difficult or time consuming; the inability to pull-it-together; restlessness with the current environment; addictive sexual behavior; negative behavior like arguing, suspicion, selfishness creates discord and damage relationships; beware of holding grudges, resentment or jealousy they will eat away at you; time to face your problems, take action and let them go; possible trouble with your mode of transportation. Are you willing to work or 'play nice' with others? Can you ask for help when you need it?

Magickal applications: for changing something quickly; for safe travel; use for binding together for a mutual cause; good luck for safe bonds in friendship; can help with finding a way to get where you want to go—even if it's just a ride to the store.

Body posture (stadha): This one takes two people or a mirror. Face each other or the mirror, standing straight. Keep your arms straight and bring them out in front of you. Place hands together in the center, stacking the palms down over top of one another.

Ehwaz represents:

- abrupt change
- partnership and cooperation, emotional commitment, ideal relationship
- power of two, twins, combination of two very different energies working harmoniously
- fertility, peace and sensuality
- the intuitive or secret force that binds together, movement in sync

Notes:

One word that sums up this Rune for me is

Mannaz (Man)   *pronounced 'MAN-naz'*

Meaning: man, humanity as a whole
Nature: masculine (originally feminine - meaning those born of woman)
Number: 20
Healing properties: remembering and aligning with the purity of innocence
Element: air
Letter: M
Sound energy: m - pronounce the letter 'm' exploring different ways to feel and say it
Color: deep red, white, green
Stone: amethyst
Trees: holly, ash, elm
Tarot association: Magician, Hanged Man
Physical: healthy connections with people or organizations
Emotional: friendship
Mental: thinking of the self as part of the whole
Spiritual: connection with spirit

Think about: the pursuance of a balanced life; teamwork lifts the burden from ones shoulders; help arrives; contact with new people that increase experience and perspective; possible distancing from family and friends over spiritual beliefs invites new positive associations; warns of possible unwise actions due to peer pressure. How well do you live and work within society? Do you enjoy connecting to healthy memories, family, friends, colleagues, spirit and important causes? What does it take to become human?

Reversed - think about: self imposed isolation or being cut off from a group; underachievement; an obstacle blocks help from coming; enemies are bothering you or you have violent feelings; immaturity and lack of insight into human nature; bad intent when working towards a goal involving desire for power, greed or sexual prowess. Do you realize your adversaries are reflecting something inside of you that you need to face and deal with? Where are you being selfish? What part of your humanity needs refinement?

Magickal applications: use when assistance from others is needed; to increase memory and intellectual power; to attract goodwill and new social contacts; good for studying; helps with psychic harmony and bringing about gifts; helps to realize your potential.

Body posture (stadha): Stand straight and lift your elbows level with your head. Cross your forearms by touching your right fingertips to your left armpit and your left fingertips to your right armpit.

Mannaz represents:

- as above, so below, the union of body, mind and spirit
- the ancestors, bloodlines, DNA
- group support assistance and advice
- memory, tradition and powers of the rational mind
- the existence of life and death in everyone makes us human

Notes:

One word that sums up this Rune for me is

Laguz (Lagus) *pronounced* 'LAH-gooz'

Meaning: water, wells, the womb the sea, lake, the balance of opposites
Nature: feminine
Number: 21
Healing properties: finding the humor in any difficulty, laughing for pleasure
Element: water
Letter: L
Sound energy: L - pronounce the letter 'L' exploring different ways to feel and say it
Color: deep green, pale blue green
Stone: malachite
Trees: willow
Tarot association: Justice, Moon, Star
Physical: sensitivity to our environment
Emotional: love
Mental: unconscious activity; dreaming
Spiritual: healing

Think about: open yourself to the waters of life that bring healing, abundance and renewal; positive things are in store for you; mental flexibility at this time will enable you to 'go with the flow'; literally taking a trip across or to the water; using your intuition to solve a problem or for inspiration; inner strength is available to overcome self-doubt; if you've chosen a spiritual path and are feeling lost, there is a need to accept the condition called the 'dark night of the soul'; time to feel your deep knowing and connect to your inner resources for wise and successful decisions; time for immersion in living life instead of evaluating, analyzing or over thinking things; the lesson of the Serenity Prayer. Are you paying attention to what you feel? Are you fluid in how you look at life?

Reversed - think about: confusion, diluted and deluded ideas; contact with a disruptive female personality (be careful not to get romantically involved); unsound ideas about yourself and others; creative blocks; deception or backstabbing from a female friend; failure to connect to your intuition; a past action may be pulling you down, clean it up. Are you being insensitive to the people or situations around you? Are you trying to take the easy way out? Are you desensitizing yourself with addictive behavior?

Magickal applications: to enhance intuitive abilities; increase vitality; helps gather energies using the will; manifest psychic abilities; helps turn the tide in your favor; healing of female related health issues; attunes unconscious desires and strengths; helps access the dream realm; use to get rid of or draw energies to you; can be used to help someone sleep and have pleasant dreams.

Body posture (stadha): Stand straight and point your arms together, straight out in front of you and slanted downward. Palms can be together, up or down; explore each way to feel which one is most aligned with your intent.

Laguz represents:

- intuition and imagination
- things unseen but felt
- initiation
- flow, life ever-flowing, wells from mother-depths of darkness, primal waters
- lunar cycle and energies, emotions
- reincarnation

Notes:

One word that sums up this Rune for me is

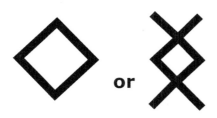

Ingwaz (Ing) *pronounced* 'ING-wahz'
Note - this Rune has two ways that it can appear

Meaning: potential, male energy
Nature: masculine
Number: 22
Healing properties: invoking and/or practicing faith
Element: water, earth
Letter: O
Sound energy: ing - keep the playful 'ng' sound going as long as possible
Color: yellow
Stone: boggart stone, ivory (even though it isn't a stone)
Trees: Apple
Tarot association: Emperor, Judgment, World
Physical: conclusion to a situation; a well deserved rest and sexual passion
Emotional: inner harmony
Mental: conclusion to a problem; a healthy outlook
Spiritual: feeling at one with the world and spirit

Think about: successful and pleasure filled activities leading to a beneficial closure of the situation or experience; a dream come true; a successful conclusion with no loose ends; freedom to pursue another direction; time to rest and gather for the fullness ahead; wonderful limitless possibilities ahead, so rest and gather your strength for it; the healthy birth of a baby; erotic love in a relationship; indicates an intuitive owl-like ability to see 360° and in the dark (the veil) at this time; a time for grounding, centering and laughing. Are you enjoying the fruits of your labor? Have you taken time to relax and celebrate?

There is no Reversed position. Think about what's hidden, unconscious or what other Runes surround it: may need to free yourself from a situation, relationship or inner rut; period before 'birthing' something new can be dangerous, align with your timing; obstacles to and/or a waste of creative energy; a sterile or unhappy love life; breaking the rules or criminal intent. Have you been closed down? - It's time to open to new things now. Are you wasting opportunities? Have you stayed somewhere too long?

Magickal applications: use as the final Rune for a successful outcome; to release energy suddenly; to bring a satisfactory ending to a cycle of events or situation; to use to 'set' a ritual so that the beneficial powers are stored; fertility; to protect a time of gestation and gathering of energies for something new; can be used to overcome physical and mental health issues; to bring safety to home or work; invokes an abundant life force; use to strengthen dreams or other workings on the astral plane.

Body posture (stadha): Stand straight, lift your arms over your head and touch your fingertips. Rotate your elbows so that they are angled out on both sides of your head. OR you can touch your fingertips together just above the pelvis with elbows out to the sides.

Ingwaz represents:

- inheritance, family heritage, inherited gifts both material and spiritual
- sexual polarity, union of opposites
- it is the end of an activity and the start of a new one
- honoring of sexuality and pleasure

Notes:

One word that sums up this Rune for me is

Dagaz (Dag)   *pronounced 'DAH-gahz'*

Meaning: day, balance
Nature: masculine
Number: 23
Healing properties: invoking and practicing hope-fullness
Element: fire, air
Letter: D
Sound energy: dhaa - dh like 'th' in the, clear with a short silence between each repetition
Color: light blue
Stone: fluorite
Trees: spruce, whitebeam oak, St. John's wort
Tarot association: Magician, Hierophant, Temperance
Physical: positive new way of living
Emotional: satisfaction
Mental: positive perspective on life
Spiritual: love and balance

Think about: a very positive and optimistic Rune for the present and future (the Runes around it show the nature of what's coming); opening to the power of transformation through your own will; personal achievement/success is now possible; being conscious is the first step in manifesting change; a new day is dawning which leads to a more prosperous life; look beyond duality for truth and meaning in life; a breakthrough towards change where things are seen from a different viewpoint; sometimes seen as a butterfly image representing the freeing of the soul to dream or even die. What are the complimentary opposites in your life (e.g. day can't exist without night)? Can you enjoy your success? Do you try to find the positive aspect of everything?

There is no Reversed position. Think about what's hidden, unconscious or what other Runes surround it: this Rune softens the impact of any reversed Runes around it; just because the change is good, don't behave recklessly (e.g. spending a ton of money because you're about to make some); can indicate depression, hopelessness or anxiety; negative outlook on life; always waiting for the 'other shoe to drop'; no light at the end of the tunnel; a need to look for a different solution to your problem; a need to 'wake-up.' Are you willing to ask for help to shed light on things you aren't seeing?

Magickal applications: use to increase finances; use to change your or someone else's attitude; to bring about a fresh start or opportunities; for invisibility; for ending things; to comfort those experiencing grief, lessen pain and cure illness; good luck charm.

Body posture (stadha): Stand straight and cross your arms in front of your chest. Rest your hands on the opposite shoulders.

Dagaz represents:

- balance, night/day, black/white, etc.
- change and evolution physically, emotionally, mentally and/or spiritually
- union of opposites, the point where duality meets, the sacred circle
- between the worlds, the place that unites

Notes:

One word that sums up this Rune for me is

Othala (Odal) *pronounced 'OH-tha-la'*

Meaning: ancestral property, land
Nature: masculine
Number: 24
Healing properties: grieving to unblock, release and make peace with life
Element: earth
Letter: O
Sound energy: oooooo – like in oath, play with the different ways to make this sound
Color: deep yellow, gold-green
Stone: petrified wood
Trees: hawthorn, oak
Tarot association: High Priestess, Empress, Moon
Physical: house; possessions; structure; grounded feeling
Emotional: feeling at home; stability
Mental: focus on creating a comforting home
Spiritual: at home with and connected to your greater self

Think about: a good home base to enjoy your family/friends, property and possessions; being moved towards environmental conservation; viewing your elders as sources of wisdom and good advice; connection with and thanking of your ancestors; inheriting property, possessions, money, stocks, a legacy, etc.; separation though severing a relationship or death; things coming full circle; the culmination of a particular stage in life; the journey always leads back to where you started. What have you claimed as your birthright? Do you take time to appreciate the gifts in your life? Do you know your gifts?

Reversed - think about: legal difficulties with land, possessions, etc.; a change in a will leaving you out or the challenging of a will; tax troubles, beware of cheating on taxes - you'll get caught; frivolous spending, no real awareness of the value of money leads to disaster; beware of gambling - you will lose; poverty, homelessness; being too miserly and not allowing abundance to enrich life; you can't buy your way out of a problem or get help from others you must stabilize your emotions to get clear and proceed. Can you let go of rigidity and invite flexibility into your attitude? Are you financially conscious?

Magickal applications: use for attracting money; for health and healing with the elderly; protection of possessions; for property matters; enhances and protects the peace security and prosperity in the home; helps draw on ancestral power; don't play around with this Rune because it can cause death if your intention is not clear; assists in grounding.

Body posture (stadha): Stand with your legs straight and spread apart. Lift your arms over your head and touch your fingers. Elbows are angled out to the sides.

Othala represents:

- inheritance of possessions, knowledge, spiritual gifts and land
- down to earth attitude toward life
- relationship with the land
- fish= end of the year eating for luck and well being
- is the never-ending fertile womb of the goddess
- loyalty to a larger group (clan, tribe, extended family, company, etc.)
- the binding of the past, present and future

Notes:

One word that sums up this Rune for me is

The Blank Rune/Wyrd* (Wurd)
pronounced 'weird'
sometimes referred to as Odin's Rune

Meaning: destiny, Wyrd
Nature: Some say masculine because of Odin. I think it's much more feminine because it's space and mystery and the cycle of birth, life, death, (re)birth. Perhaps it's both.
Healing properties: knowing the Divine within and without
Element: air
Letter: not a letter, it is the space in which anything can be
Sound energy: the absence of sound
Color: none, blue
Stone: opal, tourmaline
Trees: None. Wyrd refers to the name given to the Nornir, the three Goddesses/sisters of Teutonic Myths - Urd, Verdandi and Skuld. They each control a power of time: past, present and future. It is said that they control our fate based on our actions.
Tarot association: Fool, Emperor, Wheel of Fortune
Physical, Emotional, Mental, and Spiritual: paradox, unified & separate; fate & control over destiny

Think about: the answer is within, follow your heart, not your head; a step you are taking may be fated to change your life so that it will never be the same again (could be positive or negative or both); it may benefit you greatly to keep something secret, the timing is not right to be safe; you are not to know the answer to this question yet; decisions still need to be made before 'wise' actions can be taken. What are you allowing space for?

There is no reversed position. Think about what's hidden, unconscious or what other Runes surround it: meditate on opening to what it hidden and to move in faith from that place; look at the surrounding Runes for clues to follow a path or warnings to stop and reconsider. Have you asked spirit to help you open to your path? Have you cleaned out clutter or what isn't necessary to symbolically make space for what's coming?

Magickal applications: use this Rune before a divination to set intent: for designating time by holding it and asking that the reading cover a certain period of time (1 week, month, year, etc.); by holding it you will energetically empress upon it the wisest things for you to know from your divination

Body posture (stadha): none

*About this Rune: The blank Rune is the background that every other Rune is written on. It is a hornet's nest of controversy. Most say it is a new concept to come to the Runes by Ralph Blum in the 1980's. Others say there is evidence of this blank Rune being used as early as the 1600's for divination purposes. Rune traditionalists are outright hostile that this is being used at all. They even reduce themselves to name-calling those that do use it. So you can choose to use or not use it; your call. I use it because it is so ripe with meaning and is in sync with my beliefs.

The Norse concept of Wyrd is different than karma in that it is a personal fate in this incarnation that can't be avoided. Karma is the balancing of positive and negative acts/energy put out in many incarnations. Wyrd is the balance of those acts/energies in this life time. My understanding is that you can't avoid what you've actually created from your actions in this life. The word weird, taken from Wyrd, originally meant, 'one who believes they are in charge of their own fate.' Whether fate is because of our soul deciding before we incarnate or by our actions here, is debatable from what I've read.

Wyrd represents:

- the power of the unknowable; secrets, the sacred mysteries
- undiluted potential; simultaneously empty and pregnant
- personal destiny or fate mapped at birth that can/can't be avoided
- turning 'it' over to God/Goddess

Notes:

One word that sums up this Rune for me is _____

Web of Wyrd (Skuld's net)

Every Rune can be found in the Web of Wyrd. The Web of Wyrd, is made up of nine lines (sometimes called staves) arranged in an angular grid. It is a binding Rune that represents all possibilities for the past, present and future. A binding Rune is a combination of two or more Runes pictured as one symbol; it is used most often with magickal intent. The chart on the right displays the Runes in the order that we read – from left to right. Runes are also ordered from right to left or top to bottom. The above and the way that this book presents the Runes is the most agreed upon order (many disagree) going from left to right.

Wyrd is the Norse term for the complex and interconnecting web that binds all things together; whether those things are living, sentient, or not. The root word for Wyrd means 'worth,' 'fate,' or 'to become.' The Web of Wyrd is a reminder that all actions affect another; the actions of the past affect the present and present actions affect the future.

This web is existence; it is the action and reaction of things. By pulling on the web in one spot, pressure is created somewhere else. Our past, both our ancestry and our personal history affects us continuously. The actions that we have taken in the past as well as the actions that others have taken which have affected us in some way, contribute to who we are, where we are and what we are doing today. Every choice we make today builds upon those choices we have made in the past. The web demonstrates cyclical thinking rather than linear thinking. All timelines are inextricably interconnected- in a sense it is a representation of the tree of life.

As explained in Odin's Rune – the blank Rune – the concept of Karma helps us to understand Wyrd, but there is a major difference. Karma is concerned with multiple, past lives, while the Web of Wyrd is only concerned with this life. The 'butterfly effect' is an example of the Web of Wyrd in action. Meteorologist Edward Lorenz coined the term the 'butterfly effect' when he realized that even the tiniest motion such as the flapping of butterfly wings can caused extreme changes in weather halfway around the world. This change however in the Web of Wyrd is not limited only to the physical level, such as the weather, but can affect us on any level including emotional, mental and spiritual. This might explain some of the unpredictable behavior in our lives, as well as demonstrate the interconnectedness of all things.

In Norse mythology the web is called Yggdrasil or the World Tree. According to the Norse myths, Odin, also known as Germanic god, Wotan (god of shamans, warriors, storytellers, and seers) hangs himself from Yggdrasill seeking truth. This image represents the relationships among humanity, divinity and nature. While wounded and hanging on the World Tree, Odin discovers the secret of the Runes that allows him to be released from the tree. As he falls he grabs for the Runes hidden in the roots of the tree and is knocked unconscious; he is relieved to find them still there when he awakes.

Protecting, weaving, and shaping this web are the Nornir; three sisters similar to the Fates, their Greek cousins. Named Urd, Verdandi and Skuld, they each control a power of time: past, present and future. By controlling fate based on individual actions, the Nornir's binding Runes are so powerful that even the Aesir (the Norse gods and goddesses of war) and the Vanir (the Norse fertility gods) are subject to its constraints.

The Runes represent the shapes of the various strands of the web coming together. Every action is a strand of the web. When two or more actions/events touch, such as people meeting, fish swimming in a particular formation, people experiencing a powerful event such as an amazing live concert or a natural disaster, they meet in a particular shape. These shapes, when reduced to the simplest pattern (the crossing of web strands) that our minds can understand, are the Runes. All events are a part of the web, whether they are connections between 'living' things or not, all are represented by a Rune.

The word Rune is derived from run or runa, which means "secret" or "mystery" in Old English, Old Norse, Old German, and other Celtic and Germanic languages. Runes are a sacred concept with meanings that represent the forces of nature and the mind. This is the divination medium that seers use to communicate with the deities and the web of Wyrd for prophesying. To divine, in German (weissagen), literally means 'wise-saying.' Other legends recount that Freyja taught divination to Odin; the other Aesir Gods were not interested in learning from the Goddesses.

The Rune Magickian who works with the Runes is called the Vitki. The Vitki reads the resulting shapes of the thrown Runes and interprets their relationships to each other. In Norse Cosmology, like many shamanic indigenous people, it is believed that there is a Lower, Middle and Upper World. The interpretation of the Runes that the Vitki throws incorporates the forces acting on a situation from each of these realms. There is more on Rune spreads and uses on page 72.

The Web of Wyrd will work for you regardless of whether you're a Vitki or an average person using the Runes. You don't have to be consciously aware of a lower, middle or upper world or subtle things going on in your life to have the Wyrd work in your divination. In unseen ways, it will help to guide your way.

Ways to explore the meaning of the Web of Wyrd for you:

What random event in my past has effected the present and influences my future?

How do I feel about the idea of fate?

What is some small thing that I could change about myself or my behavior, which would put the butterfly effect to good use?
Example: I could smile a little bit more each day. I might not understand all the effects that might have, but I know it would be a change for the better.

How to Make Runes

There are only 25 Runes mentioned in this book (there are more that you may want to incorporate later). When I purchase or collect materials to make Runes, I always get 26 in case I make a mistake. There are many beautiful rituals to use when making Runes and many materials from which to make them. Wood is the traditional material to use as Odin, who is recognized as the creator of the Runes in many traditions, had two brothers that were Ash and Elm trees into which he breathed life. He also hung up-side-down from a Yew tree to gain the wisdom of the Runes. Wooden disks feel good and are easy to make Runes from in a variety of ways.

You have several choices as to what supplies to use to create your wooden Runes. My favorite is the wood-burner tool. I have made many sets for friends like this over the years.

- A wood-burner tool looks like a metal pen which you plug in that reaches temperatures of up to 950°. It sells for about $10 at a craft store such as Michael's. You simply use it like a pen; it burns the lines as you draw.

- Permanent magic marker, gel pens or paint can easily be used. You can use just one color to draw all the Runes, or you can look at the colors that the Runes align with and make your set very colorful. Gel pens can be fun because they come in sparkles.

- A set of carving knives sometimes called ciselets (small chisels) can also be used. They sell at craft stores for about $6. They come in a variety of curved, sharp ends that dig into the wood. These knives can be found next to the wood-burner tool in the store. Some say when you carve Runes you create life.
- Use a combination of the above supplies. Let your creativity take over. Craft stores also sell wooden disks for about $4 a pack... so go for it!

Wood is the traditional material used, but explore for yourself. I have seen Rune sets made from: polymer clay; similar shaped stones, shells or glass disks; fired clay; metal; cloth; cards; etc. Let your imagination be your guide.

Timing for Making Your Runes

Now that you've selected your materials, you need to think about a time to make them. Making Runes is a sacred ritual in many traditions; an auspicious time is usually chosen. These times could be: at dawn just as the sun is rising; when the sun is setting; on a Wednesday because it is Odin's day; on the day of a full moon or a new moon; or when the astrology is right. It is up to you when, how and what feels sacred or *right* in the way you make your Runes. Let intuition be your guide. Hopefully you will have so much fun doing it you'll make several sets in different ways and see what feels best.

Ritual Outline for Making Your Runes

Here is a very basic outline or formula for any ritual. Following this are examples for both a simple and complicated ritual for making Runes. Use whatever parts of each are comfortable for you. The more energy you put into the ritual preparation and process, the more powerful the ritual will be. The energy of your enjoyment during the process also contributes to the power of the ritual and your Runes.

1. **Get centered and focused** – Take a bath, meditate, dance, laugh, gather your supplies, be quiet and still, or get energized and ready.

2. **Invite Divine Energies to help** – Call in God, Guidance, Ancestors, Angels, Buddha, Rune God/Goddesses, etc., whoever you feel comfortable asking for help.

3. **State an intent/prayer** – Some people like to make an offering at this point such as lighting a candle, pouring wine, etc. The prayer or intention needs to be said out loud so you can hear the sincerity of your voice. It can sound something like this:

   • "*Hello! (Divine Energies)* this is my plan. Please bless the tools I am using to carry this out, especially my words and my hands. This is what I'd like to happen because of this ritual act (*Speak your own intention*). Please save me from any stupidity or blind spots that I have. Guide me; help me feel your loving guidance through my heart, body, mind, and Spirit. Thank you. Amen. Ashay."

   Relax, you get the picture.

4. **Do the ritual** – Make the Runes. By making the Runes in a sacred way you are actually consecrating them. You may want to add sacred actions that mean something to you

such as anointing the runes, blowing smoke into them, or speaking, singing, dancing with them. Let your imagination roam. Basically take action united with Divine Energies that you will remember. This will create a loving memory and energy that will be felt every time you use the Runes. More on consecration on page 71.

5. **Close the ritual –**
   - Thank all of the help you called in, every one of them. If you can't remember exactly who you called just add, "and anyone that my mind may have forgotten, I thank you from my heart for it always remembers."
   - Tell them why you are thankful. Hint, *because you know with their help (say what you did in the ritual today) will be for the highest good.*
   - Ask them for their continued help to take action and make choices based on what was created today.
   - Ask to be grounded and centered in the present.
   - Say "Thank You, Amen, Ashay, etc…. I now close this ritual space. "

Example of a simple ritual for making Runes:

1. Prepare a space, gather your supplies, sit down and breathe.
2. Ask for the Divine Energies to come.
3. Light a candle and ask for help to guide your hands, heart, mind, and voice so that your Runes will help guide you in making wise choices in your life.
4. Make the Runes.
5. Say thank you to the Divine Energies for helping you make such an object of beauty and wisdom. Ask the Divine Energies to help guide you whenever you use them. Thank them for grounding and centering you in the moment. Close this ritual with words such as "Namaste, Amen, Ashay, may this work be blessed."

Example of a complicated ritual for making Runes:

1. Gather your supplies and prepare a sacred space. You may want to cut your disks from a branch of a special tree (after asking permission from the Spirit of the tree, of course). Take a ritual bath before dawn, put on loose white clothing and meditate. In order to invoke Divine forces or simply act as a general invocation to the Runic powers, many Vitki perform a ritual in the four directions.

2. Ask for the Gods and Goddesses of the Runes: Odin, Balder, Freya and Freyr, the Norns, etc. and any other Divine Energy that is important to you to be present to witness and contribute their help and energy to your ritual. You may also want to invite your familial ancestors, especially those who used Magick, the ancestors of your place of birth or local land, your power animals and any other sentient beings you wish to have present.

3. Light a candle and pour a small portion of milk, apple juice or wine in offering to those Divine Energies you invited. Ask them, out loud, to guide your hands, heart, mind, and voice and lend you their powers so that your Runes will help guide you in making wise choices in your life.

4. Lay a white cloth such as a napkin or tablecloth in your sacred space to hold the finished Runes. Place your first disk on your workspace; you may want to use a clamp to hold the Runes in place as you work on them. You may choose to first lightly pencil the Runes symbols onto the wood disks, softly chanting the name of Rune as you draw it. Draw all of the lines in a downward fashion to draw energies into the Rune symbol.

Make the sign over the first disk to bless it, and speak the name of the Rune against the disk causing it to vibrate. Hold an image in your mind of the most important attribute of that Rune for you. You may also want to verbalize your intent with positive words – do not use the words 'no' or 'not' in making the Runes. While holding the image in your mind, carve, paint, or burn the Rune symbol into the disk.

When you are finished with the Rune, place it on the white cloth. After all the Runes are completed, arrange them in order. One by one, looking at each of the Runes in turn, chant or incant the name of each Rune.

5. Close the ritual. Thank all of the help you called in, every one of them. If you can't remember exactly who you called just add, "and anyone that my mind may have forgotten, I thank you from my heart for it always remembers." Tell them why you are thankful. Ask them for their continued help to take action and make choices based on what was created today. Release them. Ask to be grounded and centered in the present. Galdor the Ansuz-Laguz-Uruz formula "Ahhhluuu!" ("It is sealed"/"So mote it be") over the Rune set. Say "Thank You, Amen, Ashay, etc.... I now close this ritual space."

Consecrating Your Runes

To consecrate something is to make it sacred. If you have already made your Runes, you may have already consecrated them. Some people choose not to do a ritual when making their Runes, but do perform a ritual to consecrate them. You have already consecrated them if you made them in a ritual way. You've already made your Runes in a sacred way.

As you can imagine, there are many ways to do this. Many use their own blood, bunches of herbs, oils, or special waters, pass them through fire or fragrant smoke, run a healing peaceful energy directly into them. It is a very personal intuitive choice.

And to make it sacred is to imbue it with energy. Something sacred has energy. Something sacred usually has a powerful feeling to it. That energy is the power that someone put into it – whether by their making or their using or both.

Why do this?
- you may have Runes that someone else made that you want aligned to your energy
- you may want to deepen your relationship with your Runes
- you may want to add another layer of color or decoration
- you may just want the beauty of the experience
- you may want to participate in a group consecration and get the extra energy of support around your intent
- or you might have no interest at all. It's ok, it's not necessary.

Follow the ritual outline on page 68 to consecrate your Runes. For step 4, I like to bless them with a bit of essential oil and really enjoy their smoothness and beauty as I hold each one. Trust your intuition or just do what you enjoy; what ever you choose to do will be perfect.

Rune Spreads and Uses

There are a number of ways to draw or throw the Runes for the purpose of divination, such as drawing one Rune, three Runes, a hand full or all of the Runes. Choose the way that best suits your intention or need.

Preparing before doing a Spread

Always do some kind of prayer, ritual or invocation before reading the Runes. It wakes up your intuition and connects you to a larger perspective. To focus, one thing people sing or chant before drawing or throwing Runes is: "Runes, whisper with correct advice." After a reading, always end with a prayer of thanks and close the space.

Examples of Rune Spreads:

1. **Pull a Rune for the day** to focus your thoughts, or to give advance notice of the day's conditions or events. This single Rune will show the overall 'binding' of Wyrd involved in this situation. Since it is just one Rune, you do not have to worry about multiple interpretations causing conflicts or confusion. It is sometimes best just to ask, "Is there a place in my life right now where I could use the energy of this Rune?"

2. **Pull 3 Runes** about a situation for more interpretation and complexity.
    - one past, one present, one future *or*
    - my body, my mind, my spirit *or*
    - my family, my work, my health *or*
    - define 3 things, people or places you want to focus on

    Pull 3 Runes about a situation. The first Rune represents the factors (body, family, work, general past, etc..) that have led up to this point; the second Rune sums the situation of the (mind, health, work, general present, etc..) up at the present moment; and the third Rune represents the possible outcomes of the situation (work, spirit, health, general future, etc..). So each subsequent Rune builds upon the meaning of the previous Runes to create a more comprehensive picture of the situation.

3. **Use all (or many) of the Runes:**
    - Make an area sacred by defining the space.

    - Divide a space at least 12 x 12 inches (a bit larger is better if you have the space) into sections it can be:
      2 -representing the conscious and the unconscious;
      3 -representing the past, present, future;

4- quadrants for the emotional, mental, physical and spiritual.
*(You can also use or draw any system you are already familiar with,
such as the medicine wheel, chakra system, Tree of Life, Enneagram, etc.)*

• Draw the structure or divide into as many sections as needed. This can be done with string, tape, chalk, or paper as the dividing lines using sticky notes for the names of the sections. You can also create a cloth with paint, markers, or beads that you can unfold to use over and over.

• Reach into your bag of Runes and pull out a handful, tossing them onto your sacred area. Or you can use all of the Runes by shaking the bag or box and letting them fall where they will in that space.

• Notice which Runes are upside-down, which are hidden and which are showing or if any jump out of the space completely. Take notice as to which Runes are surrounding, touching or covering each other; these are acting more as a unit as opposed to those off by themselves. Notice which section has the most or the fewest Runes. Notice which Runes or space pulls at you from the inside.

You will begin to notice relationships. Take your time, let thoughts 'pop' into your mind, that could be your intuition speaking. Think of the one-word meanings (or look them up). Feel what seems important even if it is the blank space without Runes; that is telling you something as well. Notice the Runes that are present in the different parts of your life. Ask questions like, "What is this telling me about my (emotional, physical, spiritual, etc.) life?" "What section of this divination has the most or the least focused amount of Runes?"

Some symbolic meanings for the ways the Runes are positioned:

• **Facing up**– are ones to be conscious of; have a greater meaning in your life at the moment
• **Facing down/can't be seen**– your unconscious is at play; these Runes aren't influencing your life as much as the others
• **Upright**–a strong influence; a positive force; showing what you are conscious of or need to be aware of; the present
• **Reversed** – a strong influence that you might not be aware of; a negative force; present danger or warning
• **Turned toward the right** – you may be forcing something; too aggressive; living in the future
• **Turned toward the left** – you may not be putting enough effort into something; acting too passive; living in the past

List below some symbolic meanings you've noticed:

1. Three Runes right side up in a row –seems to consistently indicate...
Example -The past and future of the center Rune.

---

2. When a Rune(s) goes out of the designated space –seems to consistently indicate...
Example –Something I currently don't see.

---

3. When I pull the same Rune over and over –it seems to indicate...
Example –I need to ask a different question to get clarity

Some Simple Ways to Use Your Runes

Play with Your Runes: Pull the Runes from the bag or box then draw the shape of them in the air with your finger, use them in doodling, stack them in patterns, create them out of sticks on a walk in the woods, draw them in the sand or on cookies. Let your imagination go and have fun!

Walk or Carry a Rune: Pull a Rune with a question, situation or time period in mind. Hold it to your heart and focus your breathing on it while walking a labyrinth or meditating or walking in your neighborhood. It opens a way to deepen the meaning and the wisdom of what you seek.

Use a Labyrinth: Sprinkle a Labyrinth with a set of Runes facedown or randomly toss them onto a Labyrinth. As you walk the labyrinth see which Rune you are pulled to pickup. Take a moment to stop and let your body pose in the shape of the Rune. Stand and notice how you feel in the Rune shape. Ask -What does my body know when held in this form? Carry the Rune with you to look up more information after the walk. Or leave it there for someone else when walking with a group.

Keep a Rune Journal: This is a really fun and informative way to help in getting comfortable with the Runes. You can record your thoughts in the evening about how pulling a Rune at the beginning of the day helped you focus or how you felt its influence. You can record immediately after you pull the Rune to capture your first intuitions about what it is telling you. You can record larger readings, readings you do for others, insights about particular Runes and their meaning for you. You'll get to see which one comes up over and over. Great insight can come from looking at a record of your progress, your discoveries and the cycles/patterns in your life.

Ritual or Magick:
- Pick a Rune that has the qualities you desire (protection, balance, health, strength, etc.) draw them with your finger in the air in front, behind, to the right and left of you like a prayer. Then thank the forces you called upon for their aid.

- Look up which Runes have the qualities you need and make an amulet to carry or a piece of jewelry with the symbol on it to wear.

- Use the Runes that appeal to you and combine them together in a piece of art or a mandala.

- Rune binding is the construction of 2 or more Runes for use in magick or ritual. Together these Runes create a symbol that equals the sum of their parts. The Web of Wyrd is a binding Rune that contains within it every Rune. Binding is an art that is too big to address in this workbook. If this type of magick interests you, there are lots of places to explore on the web and in books.

Dreaming: Pull a Rune before bed on which to dream. Or pull one in the morning to help you interpret your dreams. Or Pull a Rune and let yourself daydream.

For Healing: Write the person's name to which you want healing energy sent, and above it write the Rune equivalent. Uses the ritual outline on page 68 and on step 4 ask the Divine to send energy to that person. Or if you are trained in the healing arts, such as Reiki or any other energy healing modality, ask the Divine to work with you to send energy for the person's highest good.

Learn the Rune Alphabet: Make a set of Runes on the back of letter tiles from the game Scrabble. Place the Rune with a marker or a wood-burning tool on the back of the related alphabetical letter. This makes learning Rune letter associations easier. Also the recognizable letters can give you a different perspective when doing a reading.

Rune Readings:

Use the following three pages to record your Rune Readings for yourself or someone else.
➔➔➔

Divination for:
Date:
Intent /Focus:

Divination for:
Date:
Intent /Focus:

Divination for:
Date:
Intent /Focus:

Rune Cheat Sheet To Keep In Your Workshop Book

In the spaces below draw each Rune, then put a couple of words that sum up their meaning for you. Use information from this book, other sources and/or your intuition.

Example: wisdom, Moveable wealth, Creative, Source Energy	13.
1.	14.
2.	15.
3.	16.
4.	17.
5.	18.
6.	19.
7.	20.
8.	21.
9.	22.
10.	23.
11.	24.
12.	25.

Rune Cheat Sheet to create on a different day Or to copy and tear out to keep with you

1.	14.
2.	15.
3.	16.
4.	17.
5.	18.
6.	19.
7.	20.
8.	21.
9.	22.
10.	23.
11.	24.
12.	25.
13.	

Example: Dianne Moore's cheat sheet; she said it was an invaluable reminder while learning. Note: everyone's cheat sheet will be different.

The Alphabet and the Runes

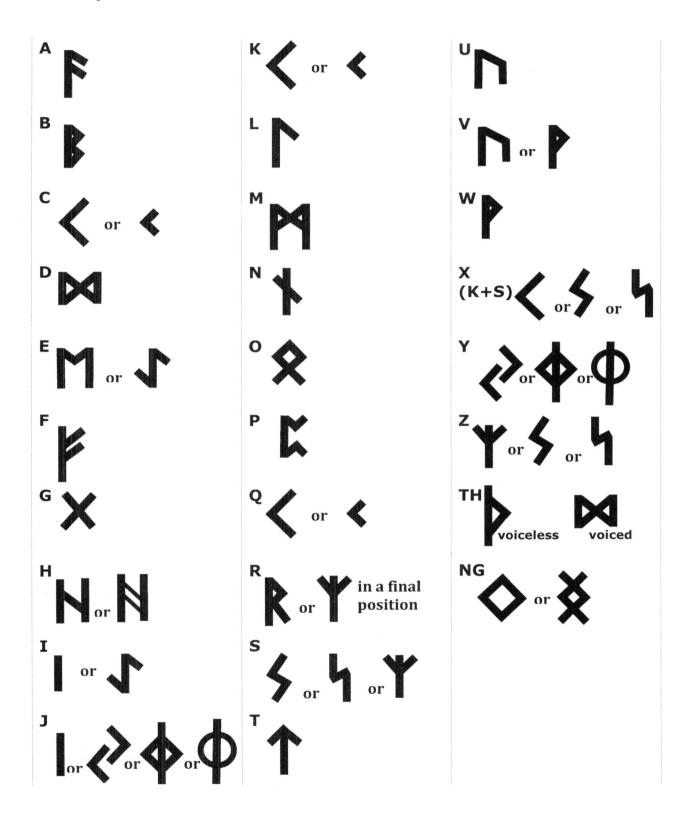

Your Name in Runes

Why do this exercise?

I have found this to be an incredibly accurate description of the challenges and of the gifts I (and family members) have inherited from our last name. It is also amazing that my first and middle names echo my nature accurately as well. The whole point is to be able to see from a different perspective. Even though you might be looking for what is familiar, the way it is combined provides a different view.

Options:

- This exercise doesn't have to all be done in one sitting. You could do it on a different day and get something different.
- You can use this for naming a company or figuring out the meaning of a company you work for.
- You can do one for your friend and have your friend do yours,

1. Write your <u>full name</u> with Runes (use page 93).
Note: Runes can be written left to right, right to left, bottom up or top down; you choose.

Example 1:
(make sure to use your full name; I've used just my last name to give you an idea)

H   a   l   l   s

2. Write a summary of your name. Using your cheat sheet, find each letter of your first and last name, noting the meaning of each Rune. Choose the meaning of each Rune by picking the word that feels best for you. If there are two Rune letters that represent one of the letters in your name, pick the one that intuitively feels right. If you have a TH in your name try using T and H or TH. Play with it. Nothing is right or wrong. Same with NG.

Then go back and read the "Think About" section of each Rune or add what you know about the words that you picked. Oftentimes people try to include too much information. When you begin, just add everything that speaks to you. Whatever has an impact on you, note it. Go for what you recognize in you in the Runes. Then hone it down.

Example 2:

H	a	l	l	s
Hail	God	Water	Water	Sun

Below I have written one sentence for each letter that sums up the meaning for me now; it may change in time. Since I have 2 L's I wrote just one sentence but know it has extra emphasis.

Through disruption a path is created between the 2 worlds which allows transformation to occur. Spirit comes to connect through intuition. Through Will and conscious intent Spirit/Positive Energies are invited to flow though this life. A willingness and intent to do positive work and bring light in the world is the key.

3. Write what you must watch out for:
Read the "Reversed" meaning section of each Rune to help you with this step.

Example 3:

H	a	l	l	s
Hail	God	Water	Water	Sun

There is one sum-up sentence for each letter.

Freezing in inflexible controlling ways can sever the connection to the Divine and leave blocks to stop progress. If this occurs decisions can be hard to make because they can't be felt. Negative thinking can take over and help to dig a deeper hole to be lost in. You will remain in the dark until you can be open to receive help.

Complete the exercise on page 93.

1. Write your <u>full name</u> with Runes
Note: Runes can be written left to right, right to left, bottom up or top down.

2. Go though letter by letter using your cheat sheet and write a summary of your name using the meanings of the Runes. (Use the "Think About" section of each Rune)

3. Write what you must watch out for. (Use the "Reversed" section of each Rune)

Use the back of this page if needed.

Runes in a Therapeutic Setting
By Dianne Moore, M.ED.,MFT

In his book, *Man and His Symbols*, C.G. Jung speaks of our being able to achieve wholeness only through knowledge and acceptance of our unconscious minds. Jung spent most of his life doing just this...delving into his own mind and looking for new ways to understand himself. I don't believe we can do more with our own lives than coming to a place where we feel we truly understand ourselves. Throughout his life, Jung used many different tools to accomplish this, but he especially loved using symbols as the pathway to his inner psyche.

The Runes were my first encounter with the magic of working with symbols, and I would like to share with you some of my early experiences with them.

Twenty something years ago, I accepted a job as a counselor at The Relatives Adolescent Crisis Shelter in the Dilworth area of Charlotte, and my life was changed entirely. I began to move in a totally new direction with my thinking, and I am still moving in that new direction.

I learned so much from those young people, and one of those I learned from was Bernie; a very smart 15 year old who went through our residential program several times. I had the good fortune of being his counselor. He is a happy adult today who works in the NC Mountains as a park ranger. Bernie's family situation had become difficult, and he needed guidance, but he had no trouble looking into himself for guidance. He was confident and peaceful, not something we saw much of at the runaway shelter. Bernie was not very religious, and I was curious as to where he drew his obvious strength. When I asked him what motivated him to work so hard on himself, he told me about his little bag of Runes that he carried on his belt at all times. I was fascinated with Bernie's bag of symbols, as were the other residents of the shelter, so I asked him to help me make my own. I was working with a potter's wheel at home at the time, so I brought some clay, carved the 24 symbols into the little pieces in the energy of the rising sun (at Bernie's direction), then fired them in the oven in the big kitchen of The Relatives. After this little bit of work on my part, the Runes took over, and have amazed me over and over again since.

The children and teens in our residential setting were usually in serious trouble, with many complex problems. It was difficult to get them to work close to their issues, as they were so emotionally potent, and they usually had very few skills for moving through problems without getting stuck. The Runes came at a perfect time for me, as they allowed the kids to be somewhat removed from their trauma as they "played" with the symbols and tried to move forward with their young lives through difficult, often traumatic circumstances.

Each night after dinner, we conducted a house meeting around the big oak table in the kitchen. This was where I first introduced the Runes to the residents, and it was powerful from the beginning. Bernie had moved on with his life, but I had my own copy of Ralph Blum's, *The Book of Runes*, and I had used them myself for months, so I was confident that they would be helpful to the kids. I was right. I tossed my bag of Runes to the middle of the table and asked, "Who would like to start?"

I did not often have to ask a child to talk to me after that, I just got out my bag of Runes, and the child's curiosity and the power of the Rune symbols took over. I just listened. These young people were already overwhelmed by the complexities of their lives, and were not at all interested in complex ways of working with their issues. I found them to be enthralled by the Runes, and the magic of looking at the symbols as they related to their lives. They talked much more intimately about their lives when they had a Rune to hold on to, and most often moved out of their stuckness.

With adolescents, my methods of working with the Rune symbols were extremely intuitive and simple. Usually I would ask the child if he/she had a preferred way of casting the Runes. For example sometimes a child would want to pick three Runes for guidance around his past, present or future. Other times they might want to throw the whole bag and do a spread; some even danced with them. However, if they could not decide, I would ask them to pick just one Rune from the bag. We would then read from our cheat sheet, and they would respond to the question, "Is there a place in your life right now where you could use the energy of this Rune?" The most common response in my ten years at the shelter was... the child would get very quiet, lower his head and wipe his eyes with his sleeve before answering my question. I eventually introduced a Rune journal, and the residents would learn to write about their issues before being able to talk about them. Some of the deepest and most profound psychological movement I have ever witnessed occurred around that big oak table at The Relatives between a bag of Rune symbols and a severely disturbed adolescent.

After experiencing such success with the Runes at the shelter, the staff wanted to make their own. We baked almost as many Runes as we did cookies in those days. The counselors devised many more ways of using the Runes, more complex and interesting, but never better. Some of the folks I worked with still call occasionally, and some are still using them for their personal growth. I also gave several family members the experience of making Rune stones from small quartz stones I found on the beaches of the Outer Banks of NC. My sister says she sometimes still will pick a stone and carry it in her pocket all day to help her process a certain issue.

I learned that a Ralph Blum book, a cheat sheet, a bag of handmade Runes, and a nice Rune journal made a wonderful gift for family or friends. I learned to give them after loosing many a set after family visits. Inevitably, where ever I went the Runes were a big hit, spurring many interesting conversations.

The cheat sheet evolved from a small piece of paper that I kept on my clipboard at The Relatives (shown on page 87) to remind me of the meanings of the Runes before I had familiarized myself with them. After reading many books about the Runes and realizing the meanings can be somewhat ambiguous, my meanings came mostly from working with the kids. These seemed to be the meanings which best served our intentions with the residents. We mostly wanted to encourage them to talk about themselves in a proactive manner, and the Runes worked.

I am so happy to be able to contribute to the *Rune Workshop* workbook as Jennifer's enthusiasm has reignited my own fascination with the Rune symbols. I never expected the book to be of this quality and I am so pleased that it is because it will be useful to anyone who wants to use it for self growth. I wish I had it 20 years ago! I am sure it will be helpful to you if you follow these symbols into your own lives.

I remembered this morning that my lifetime Runes are Isa and Kano. I still need the energy of these symbols in my life today. Be still, and open. Lifetime Runes come from your journal; at some point you will realize that 2 or 3 Runes keep showing up over time for you. You will intuitively know after awhile that these Runes are meant for you to keep working with. They can also appear in different ways; every time I walk on the beach I see Isa and Kano (also known as Kenaz or Cen) in the lines of sand or on shells. As with dreams the images just appear and usually I can make an association where the energy of that Rune can be useful. Not always quickly or simply but ideally the association will manifest and be helpful in my everyday life. So please pull the Runes, journal about them and enjoy the journey to your unconscious mind!

Leanne

Rune Resources

There is a lot of information available on the Runes. I used what resonated for me; I encourage you to find what works for you. This book was compiled from the knowledge of my friend Dianne Moore, my observations & intuition and the following sources:

The Book of Runes by Ralph Blum
The Cabalistic Correspondence Cards by Lance Reynard
Discovering Runes by Bob Oswald (beautifully illustrated- includes associated gods and astrological correspondence)
The Element Encyclopedia of Secret Signs and Symbols by Adele Nozedar
Futhark: A Handbook of Rune Magic by Edred Thorsson
The Healing Runes by Ralph Blum and Susan Loughan
The Magical Language of Runes by P.M.H. Atwater
Rune Mysteries by Silver RavenWolf and Nigel Jackson
The Runes by Lisa Peschel
The Runes and Their Meaning by Greenwoman Crafts
Taking up the Runes by Diana L. Paxson
Understanding the Runes by Michael Howard
The Woman's Book of Runes by Susan Gray

These web locations were used for information on the blank Rune and the Web of Wyrd:

http://www.metta.org.uk/Runes/allRunes.asp

http://www.octavia.net/anglosaxon/Wyrd.htm

This site has a FREE! Rune Converter that gives you a choice of five systems of Germanic Runic writing to convert modern English into. I used it to convert the Albert Einstein and Mother Meera quotes in this book into the Elder Furthark Runes.

http://www.vikingrune.com

About Joanne Brunn

Joanne Brunn, Ph.D. brings a fresh perspective to leaders and organizations wishing to initiate, embrace, and sustain change. Her research and experience with collaborative creativity, intuition, innovative leadership, and integrative thinking has resulted in her multi-disciplinary approach to organizational challenges and transformational change.

She has studied human capacities development and innovative leadership strategies under Dr. Jean Houston, a founder of the human potential movement and leader in cultural development initiatives.

She is the author of *Bridging the Gap: Exploring Indigenous and Western Student's Experiences in an Indigenous Perspectives Cultural Immersion Program* (UMI, 2006); *Awakening Your Psychic Skills: Using Intuition to Guide your Everyday Life* (Barrons Educational Series, 2004); and *Aphrodite's Secrets: Dressing Up for Getting Down and Other Ways to Unleash Your Inner Sex Goddess* (Fair Winds Press, 2004).

Through work with Sobonfu Some, from the Dagara, an Indigenous tribe in Burkina Faso, West Africa, she has learned how ancient wisdom teachings can expand and deepen our understanding and usage of integrative thinking approaches and creativity.

She is currently enjoying working with a start-up software company, being a part-time professor at Saybrook University as a faculty advisor in the Creativity Studies program, and creating mobile apps to develop one's creative thinking.

About Dianne Moore

Dianne Moore, M.ED., MFT has worked as a counselor in North and South Carolina for over twenty years. Nine of those years as a counselor and clinical supervisor at The Relatives, and fifteen years with her private psychotherapy practice in Charlotte, NC and Van Wyck, SC.

A head on automobile collision five years ago caused her to give up her private practice. She now facilitates workshops on issues such as 'aging wisely' and 'dancing with our issues, dream images and insights'.

Dianne trained with Francene Shapiro in EMDR, and she has been certified in Control Theory, Reality Therapy and several nontraditional therapies. She is a certified practitioner of the internationally known Trager Approach to mind/body work. She has worked in the areas of woman's issues, trauma, and mind/body issues, and is anticipating learning much more as she approaches her seventieth year on this good earth.

She likes the reciprocity and growth that occurs naturally in groups. "Let's pool our resources and go forward."

About the Author Jennifer Halls

Jennifer Halls is an expert at helping people discover, own and use their intuition. As a fulltime consultant and teacher, she has led thousands of sessions to help clients experience, understand and navigate their inner-guidance. Her methods are straightforward, practical and fun because Jennifer believes intuition is a natural part of a normal and happy life.

For more than 25 years she has been fascinated with the Runes, the Tarot and many other oracular tools. They have taught her that the power in any complex system comes from finding its simplicity. The key to that discovery is to not be intimidated by the complexity but to enjoy playing with the system. Creating fun and simple ways to discover and engage our inner knowing is at the core of her work.

Learning has been Jennifer's lifelong partner. She was ordained in 1998 by Rev. Rosalyn Bruyére; initiated in the Dagara system by Sobonfu Somé in 2004; and certified by Lauren Artress as a Veriditas labyrinth facilitator in 2011. She is dedicated to using a wide variety of ways and tools to help people develop and rely on their intuition.

South Carolina is her home. There she shares a Charleston style house with her journalist husband Michael and their big black dog, Louise. Between sessions with clients, she writes, paints and harbors secret desires for buttered popcorn, Blenheim hot ginger ale and sensational novels.

ᛗᚨᚲᛖ ᛁᛏ ᚨ ᚺᚨᛒᛁᛏ ᛏᛟ ᚨᛊᚲ ᚦᛖ
ᛞᛁᚹᛁᚾᛖ ᚠᛟᚱ ᛖᚹᛖᚱᛃᚦᛁᛜ

Make it a habit to ask the Divine for everything. ~ Mother Meera

Printed in Great Britain
by Amazon